Top
DANCE
Tips

JEN JONES

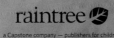

raintree

a Capstone company — publishers for children

Raintree is an imprint of Capstone Global Library Limited, a company incorporated in England and Wales having its registered office at 264 Banbury Road, Oxford, OX2 7DY – Registered company number: 6695582

www.raintree.co.uk
myorders@raintree.co.uk

Edited by Gena Chester
Designed by Veronica Scott
Picture research by Eric Gohl
Production by Steve Walker
Originated by Capstone Global Library LTD
Printed and bound in China

ISBN 978 1 4747 3720 3
20 19 18 17 16
10 9 8 7 6 5 4 3 2 1

British Library Cataloguing in Publication Data
A full catalogue record for this book is available from the British Library.

Acknowledgements
We would like to thank the following for permission to reproduce photographs: Alamy: Danita Delimont, 18, Gregg Vignal, 29, Michael Dwyer, 26; Capstone Studio: Karon Dubke, 6 (bottom), 7, 9, 14, 15, 17, 20, 22, 23; Newscom: Sipa USA/John Salangsang, 13 (right), ZUMA Press/Ricky Fitchett, 5; Shutterstock: cover, 1, 6 (top), 10 (top), 32, antoniodiaz, 21 (inset), Comaniciu Dan, 12, DavidTB, 25, Evgeny Karandaev, 21 (computer), Jiri Hera (floor background), Mihai Blanaru, 11, Monkey Business Images, 27, pio3, 16 (right), rozaliabelle, 4 (curtain), Tyler Olson (ballet bar background), Undrey, 10 (bottom), Vagengeim, 19 (all), yamix, 13 (left), 16 (left)

We would like to thank Kelsey Chester for her invaluable help in the preparation of this book.

CONTENTS

Get into the groove

Audience members were on the edge of their seats as they watched America's most famous ballerina, Misty Copeland, at the Detroit Opera House. She performed the role of Princess Florine in 2016 and dazzled the crowd in a sky blue tutu. She soared with graceful turns, leaps and lifts.

Copeland has proved that hard work and talent can take you far in the dance world. From the ballet studio to the ballroom to the streets, you'll find beginners, pros and everyone between. While each type of dance has a unique approach and feel, there are basic skills that all dancers must learn.

Misty Copeland also performed at the
Marian Anderson Award Gala.

Chapter 1

DANCE *basics*

People dance in hundreds of different styles all over the world. Though the list is long, several main styles of dance stand out among the rest. Here's a quick need-to-know rundown.

BALLET: If you've ever seen The Nutcracker or Swan Lake, you've seen ballet at its finest. This classical art form is highly structured and known for graceful, flowing movements. Ballerinas dance in special shoes on their toes, or en pointe.

BALLROOM: Ever hear the saying, "It takes two to tango?" The tango, waltz and foxtrot are all types of ballroom dances. Each type is a social dance that relies on partnering.

JAZZ: This type of dance is almost always performed on stage, either during dance competitions or musical theater. Jazz developed from stage, ballroom and African dances during the 1800s and 1900s. Some jazz routines are theatrical performances with comedic or overly dramatic movements.

TAP: Footwork combinations create the **rhythm** in tap dancing. This is thanks to special shoes with loud metal plates on the heels and toes.

---

rhythm regular beat in music, poetry, or dance

lyrical style of dance that mixes ballet technique with modern style; lyrical moves are fluid and expressive

break dancing very energetic and acrobatic form of dance in which dancers touch the ground with their hands, heads, and feet

CONTEMPORARY: Contemporary combines different types of dance, such as jazz, ballet and **lyrical** to create a diverse, creative style. This challenging style is very popular in the competition scene.

HIP-HOP: Hip-hop got its start in the Bronx, a neighborhood in New York City. The style focuses on creative freestyle moves. A popular style of hip-hop is **break dancing**.

GETTING *in step*

Not sure where to start? The great news is that anyone can learn to dance. And there are lots of places to learn. Some schools have dance teams. They may hold auditions for people interested in joining. Many dancers attend dance studios. These studios offer many levels for every type of dancer. Some dancers want to dance just for fun, while others train for competitions. No matter what skill level, you're bound to find classes that are right for you.

Find the rhythm

Dancers don't just hear music. They feel it too. Thanks to a keen sense of **musicality**, dancers are able to create a matching rhythm with their bodies.

But what if you're a bit offbeat? The good news is that you can improve your sense of rhythm. One easy way to practise is to clap or tap a pencil along to music. Try using songs of different **tempos** to see how rhythms and timing can vary. Recruit a more musical friend or your dance teacher to make sure you're staying on the beat.

~ Tip ~

Skipping with a rope along to music will help you follow the beat. Plus, it's great exercise!

Stretch into success

Before any class or performance, dancers prepare their bodies with a series of stretches. Not only does this prevent injuries, but it also boosts flexibility. Flexibility gives dancers a better range of motion. This can lead to higher jumps and kicks, cleaner lines and wider **turnouts**.

Dancers do two types of stretches to prepare for their movements. Dynamic stretches keep your body moving. Static stretches stay in one place. An example of dynamic stretching would be doing a series of grand **pliés** at the ballet barre. A static stretch might be doing a split. Experts suggest holding a static stretch for at least 30 seconds to get the best benefits.

A BREATH OF *fresh air*

Proper breathing will increase the effectiveness of any stretch. Inhale slowly through your nose. Hold your breath for a bit, and then exhale through your nose or mouth. Make sure to breathe from your stomach, rather than from your chest. You should be able to see your belly going in and out. Breathe out as you move more deeply into the stretch.

musicality sensitivity to, knowledge of, or talent for music

tempo speed or timing of a musical piece

turnout rotation of a dancer's legs from the hips

plié ballet move where the knees bend while the torso is help upright; grand pliés require a deep bend in the knees

More power for you

To master the athletic side of dance, building stomach, or core, strength is a must. Strength training helps dancers control their movements. It also creates a stable centre for balancing. Many dancers do **Pilates**, yoga or ballet barre workouts to build up their core power.

Plank

This simple exercise strengthens your upper body, chest and core. Go into a modified press-up position with your weight on your forearms. Keep your body in a straight line and your stomach muscles tight. Hold the position for at least 30 seconds. As you get stronger, work up to holding a plank for two minutes.

Pilates exercise program that helps tone muscles and strengthen the body's centre

Superman

It's a bird, it's a plane … it's an awesome strength exercise! The Superman works both your back and core muscles. To do it, lie flat on your stomach with your legs straight and arms extended out past your head. Raise your left leg and your right arm at the same time, while also lifting your head. Lower back to the ground. Repeat, lifting your right leg and your left arm. Finally, lift both legs and both arms at the same time. Do this sequence 20 times.

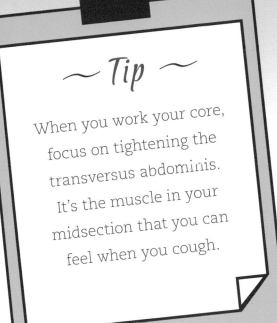

~ Tip ~

When you work your core, focus on tightening the transversus abdominis. It's the muscle in your midsection that you can feel when you cough.

Chapter 2

ALL THE
right moves

It's your turn

No matter what type of dance you're doing, turns are bound to be part of it. Just ask a ballerina, who turns en pointe. Some turns travel across the floor. Others, such as **pirouettes**, stay in one spot.

To do a pirouette, start with your arms in an "L" shape. Your left arm should be straight in front of you and your right arm out to the side. Step back with your left leg into a plié. Push off your left foot and bring it to your opposite knee. Lift your right foot onto the ball of your foot. Move your arms into an "O" position, using them to guide your body into a clockwise, also called en dehors, full turn.

~ *Tip* ~

For better turns, press down into the floor with your supporting leg. This creates a sturdier platform to turn, which gives you more balance.

pirouette

pirouette one-legged turn on the ball of the foot or on the tip of the toe in pointe shoes

ROUND AND *round*

As you get better at your turn technique, you can increase the number of rotations you do. For inspiration, look no further than young Sophia Lucia. At age 10, she broke the Guinness World Record in 2013 by doing 55 pirouettes in a row. Sophia accomplished this dizzying feat by spotting.

Spotting is a technique that prevents dizziness and helps propel your body around. Choose a focus point in front of you and train your eyes on it. As soon as your head needs to turn, whip around to face the focus point again. Continue as many times as needed for the number of turns.

Taking the leap

Want to take your dancing to the next level? Jumps and leaps are featured in almost every type of dance. For instance, a ballerina might execute a leap called a jeté. A jazz dancer might rock an airborne turn with bent legs. This is a barrel jump. And that's just the beginning! The list of jumps and leaps across dance styles is practically endless!

A dancer executing a ring leap.

Jumps and leaps can be done in place or while moving. Both types require strength to perform. Moving can help a dancer build more **momentum**. With either type, it's important to do a plié when launching and landing. Not only will this protect your knees, but it will also improve your jump by leaps and bounds.

~ *Tip* ~

Add height by doing **plyometric** exercises. Tuck jumps are a great example. Start in a low squat, with your hips below your knees. Jump as high as you can, bringing your knees into your chest. Return to a low squat position, and repeat.

momentum force or speed created by movement

plyometric exercise involving repeated jumping to increase muscle power

Kick up a fuss

Ballerinas raise their back legs into graceful **arabesques**. Hip-hop dancers launch their bodies back onto all fours before doing powerful hinge kicks. No doubt about it – kicks, or battements, are a key part of any dancer's toolbox.

Typically, you should keep your legs as straight as possible in a kick. Toes can be either pointed or flexed, depending on the desired effect. Pointed toes are a staple in ballet. Flexed toes are usually found in hip-hop and contemporary dance styles.

arabesque ballet move where a dancer stands on one leg and extends the other behind

A sauté arabesque, like the one shown here, is done in the air.

Tight hamstrings are the enemy of high kicks. Try stretching to maximize your leg height. Lie down on the floor with both legs out in front of you. Draw your left knee in towards your chest. Then extend and straighten the leg. Hold your leg behind the calf or thigh, and pull it gently towards your nose. Hold the stretch for 30 seconds. Repeat with your right leg.

~ Tip ~

Want to move your kicks into high gear? Work on your splits! When your body can achieve the splits, you automatically have a larger range of motion for kicks.

Chapter 3

TAKE IT TO THE
next level

Ask any pro how she got to the top of her game, and training will likely be her answer. Though it may seem obvious, taking classes is a dancer's route to success. Some dancers choose to cross-train across different genres. Others choose a specific focus like tap or hip-hop.

Most experts agree that learning ballet provides the foundation for great technique. Not only does the classical genre improve form and posture, but it also prepares dancers for other styles. The five ballet foot positions are found throughout jazz and contemporary dance.

IN *position*

THE FIVE BALLET FOOT POSITIONS ARE:

1ST POSITION

1ST POSITION: Heels touch with toes turned out — from the hip, not the knees.

2ND POSITION

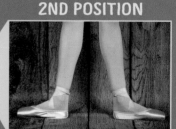

2ND POSITION: Feet should be about hip-width apart with toes turned out.

3RD POSITION

3RD POSITION: Draw one foot towards the other, so that its heel touches the middle of the other foot.

4TH POSITION

4TH POSITION: Step forwards with the front foot, keeping your feet turned out. To make sure you're doing it right, start in fifth position and draw the front foot forwards from there.

5TH POSITION

5TH POSITION: Turn feet out from the hips. With one foot in first position, bring the other foot directly in front of the first. Heels should be resting next to toes for both feet.

Chapter 4

WE GOT
the beat

Dance routines are like snowflakes – all of them are unique in their own way. So what sets each routine apart? Choreography. Whether taking the stage solo or with a group, choreography provides the framework to bring artistry to life.

Memorizing and mastering choreography can be difficult. Some choreographers use counts to mark each move; others make sounds that mimic each beat. Many routines are strung together by "8-counts," which break down moves into smaller chunks for easy learning.

Memorize the moves

If your mind goes blank every time you try to memorize a new dance routine, don't stress! There are many tricks you can try.

• Try giving steps nicknames that will help you remember the sequence. For instance, if a move reminds you of digging soil, call it that.

• Take a video of your dance teacher demonstrating it so you can review whenever you're stuck.

• Use moments of downtime to run through the routine in your head. The more time you spend thinking about it, the easier it will become.

• Practising the routine over and over again can wear you out. Try marking instead. While marking, dancers substitute full movements of a routine for smaller representations. A turn in a routine could be a finger twirl in marking.

Footloose and fancy free

Ever hear the phrase, "Think on your feet?" Freestyling gives it a whole new meaning! In freestyle, dancers **improvise**, letting the music lead the way.

Getting started is simple: turn on the tunes! Listen to different styles of music, from rap to country, and see what types of movement come naturally. Though it may feel a bit awkward at first, try not to hold yourself back. Just keep moving, and you'll get better! Use a mirror or record a video of yourself as you dance. This can help provide insight into what moves work best.

~ Tip ~

Not sure where to start? Work on your musicality. Clapping or clicking your fingers to the beat will help you feel the music more. Once you've mastered rhythm, you're more likely to move with ease.

improvise to make up on the spot

Unique to you

Creativity is a key part of freestyle. But everyone's creative process is different. Some dancers work best in a studio with mirrored walls. Others like to find inspiration out in public. So how do you find out what works for you? Practise!

Practising choreography might not seem like the best way to freestyle. But more practice brings more confidence in a dancer's ability. With practice, a dancer becomes comfortable with a wide range of moves, which increases the variety in his or her freestyle.

Dancers develop their style the more they practise. They take note of which moves they favour and how they interpret the music. Where one dancer may approach a song with hard-hitting moves at a fast pace, another might demonstrate strong, graceful lines. Interpretation, depth of knowledge, and creativity combine to create a unique freestyle routine for each person.

~ Tip ~

The best way to spark creativity is to break free of your routine. Go to an art show or take a class that's out of your comfort zone.

Chapter 5

TAKING
centre stage

When performers such as Beyoncé storm the stage, people can't take their eyes off them. They've got that "it" quality, or stage presence. They have the ability to command a crowd's attention and leave them wanting more.

For dancers, the magic lies in the way they connect to the audience, the music and the choreography. To make that connection, dancers rely on emotion and energy. They translate the music and its message through facial expressions, body movements and eye contact. Channelling the right energy also helps set the tone. A lyrical routine might call for a soft, reflective feel. A break-dancing routine is likely to be more energetic with pops of moves.

As a dancer, you can choose music and moves that play to your strengths. If you have a bubbly personality, an upbeat, catchy jazz number can highlight your charm. If your dance teacher is always complimenting your clean lines, a contemporary routine could be the way to go.

~ Tip ~

Take acting classes to learn how to better tap into your emotions and feel more at home onstage.

Grace under pressure

What do ballerina Misty Copeland and ballroom dancer Julianne Hough have in common? They've both struggled with stage fright. In fact, many dancers deal with pre-performance nerves. If you're one of them, don't worry! There are lots of ways to tame those butterflies.

Consider creating a pre-show ritual. Self-affirmations, or positive statements said to yourself, will help get you in the right mindset for a performance. Other good techniques include deep breathing exercises, listening to calming music and **visualization**.

Sometimes, just going through the motions is a good thing! Practising your complete routine the day of a performance can be exhausting on the brain and the body. Instead, dancers mark their routine.

visualization act of imagining or forming a mental picture

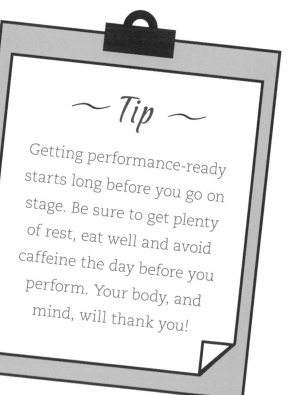

~ Tip ~

Getting performance-ready starts long before you go on stage. Be sure to get plenty of rest, eat well and avoid caffeine the day before you perform. Your body, and mind, will thank you!

A ballerina takes her final bow as the audience applauds.

Always remember that practice makes perfect. And if you do make a mistake during a performance, don't worry! Dedication, along with a few tips, will help in whatever dance path you choose.

GLOSSARY

arabesque ballet move where a dancer stands on one leg and extends the other behind

break dancing very energetic and acrobatic form of dance in which dancers touch the ground with their hands, heads, and feet

improvise to make up on the spot

lyrical style of dance that mixes ballet technique with modern style; lyrical moves are fluid and expressive

momentum force or speed created by movement

musicality sensitivity to, knowledge of, or talent for music

Pilates exercise program that helps tone muscles and strengthen the body's centre

pirouette one-legged turn on the ball of the foot or on the toes in pointe shoes

plié ballet move where the knees bend while the torso is held upright; grand pliés require a deep bend in the knees

plyometric exercise involving repeated jumping to increase muscle power

rhythm regular beat in music, poetry, or dance

tempo speed or timing of a musical piece

turnout rotation of a dancer's legs from the hips; an ideal turnout is 180 degrees

visualization act of imagining or forming a mental picture

FIND OUT MORE

Dance (Mad About), Judith Heneghan (Wayland, 2016)

Street Dance (Radar), Liz Gogerly (Wayland, 2013)

Impressive Dance Moves (Try This at Home) Ellen Labrecque (Raintree, 2014)

WEBSITES

http://www.onedanceuk.org/
Find out about all the styles of dance practised in the United Kingdom.

http://artsalive.ca/en/dan/dance101/facts.asp
Fantastic facts about different styles of dance.

INDEX